CHILDREN IN LENT

In memory of Sandra Hughes
a wonderful friend and spiritual companion

Anne Marie Lee

Children
in Lent

A RESOURCE BOOK FOR
HOME, SCHOOL AND PARISH

the columba press

First published in 1996 by
the columba press
93 The Rise, Mount Merrion, Blackrock, Co Dublin

Cover by Bill Bolger
Illustrations by Elaine Wisdom and Berni Clarke
Additional text by Sean McEntee
Printed in Ireland by Colour Books Ltd, Dublin

ISBN 1 85607 160 X

Contents

Introduction

Lent lasts for forty days and nights, not including Sundays. It's a long time. I have written this book with the assistance of a number of people to help you to keep children focused on Jesus during Lent in a way that will be attractive to them. There are themes, prayers, stories, games, crafts and pictures to colour for each week, and there is the Easter Garden project which will take about six weeks to complete. Maybe Lent will seem too short when you get involved with these activities!

Lent begins on Ash Wednesday and finishes on Holy Saturday. Ash Wednesday is so-called because you will see people going around with blobs of black ash on their foreheads. This is a reminder that we came from dust and we will go back to dust. We only need our bodies for this earth. In the next life with God we will be spirit. The ashes used on this day are made by burning the palm branches that were used on Passion Sunday last year.

Ash Wednesday and Good Friday are days of fast and abstinence. Abstinence means voluntarily to do without something we like. Denying ourselves something that we would like to have is good for us. It helps strengthen our character, to be strong and to say no when we are tempted to do something we know is wrong. Some children give up things like sweets, cakes or comics. Whatever way you choose to encourage the children to keep Lent this year, I hope this book will be a help to you in nourishing their spiritual lives.

How to use this book

This book is written for parents, teachers and lay ministers working with children of Primary School age. It is a resource book written specifically for Lent but which can be dipped into at any time of the year, for example, for one-day retreats. The contents can be adapted to suit the age and understanding of the children you are working with.

The idea is to focus on a different theme each week and choose activities that link into the theme. I have linked up a set of activities for each week which you can follow or you can dip into the book as you like.

The Easter Garden is the background project of the book. It is constructed week by week by the children, keeping them in mind of the events of Jesus' life, especially in those last weeks before his death. The visual impact of the events from Good Friday to Easter Sunday, as played out by the figures in the garden, will remain etched on the minds of the children, just as the events surrounding the birth of Jesus are because of the crib, the star and the three wise men.

The *Field Trip* should be the first activity, as its purpose is to encourage the children to think about God and creation, and also to collect the materials for the book marker, which will take three weeks to prepare, as well as items for the Easter Garden. If you are working with children who are new to you, this is also a good opportunity to bond with them.

The *Themes* are written to be read to the children and discussed with them. To do this, I suggest the children sit in a circle on the floor with some lighted candles in the centre. Read the theme slowly, follow it with discussion, and close with some prayers. Allow the discussion to flow, even if it goes off the immediate track. Children need to have their story heard.

Some of the *Prayers* were written by the children of the fourth class in Archbishop McQuaid Primary School in Loughlinstown, Co Dublin. They could be read by the children themselves, who might then like to think about them. Encourage the children to write some prayers of their own. You may like to use the prayers after the reading of the stories as well.

The *Stories* relate to the six themes and are written to stimulate the imagination of the children, with plenty of strong concrete images which help to convey the meaning of the theme in practical terms.

The *Games* I chose because they can be a focus of discussion on how we behave towards one another, while at the same time being great fun. Asking the children how they felt, being restricted by the rules of the particular game, helps them to get in touch with their feelings of frustration, anger, annoyance, satisfaction and joy, while communicating and co-operating with others.

The doing of *Crafts* can be spun out over the week to give the children a sense of anticipation and delayed gratification. Pick and choose the crafts you want to do with the children at this stage, as it is unlikely that you will have time to do all of the crafts in the six weeks.

A field trip

Take the children out on a field trip in the week on which Ash Wednesday occurs, preferably on a dry day. The group going out should be armed with plastic bags and a large heavy book – ideally a telephone directory – or, if you are lucky enough to have one, a flower press.

If you are based in the city, go to the local park, common or woods. If you are in the country you have a wider choice of places to go.

Help the children to wonder at God's creation, at the way nature works, its harmony and the colour combinations which never seem to clash. For example, talk to them about the trees – how the oak tree provides the squirrel with winter food. It is home to the birds who nest in its branches and to millions of insects and creepy crawlies, some of which are food for the birds. Trees, including the oak, soak up water from the ground, especially after heavy rainfall and help to keep it dry. Oak trees are cut down and made into furniture by carpenters and cabinet makers and this furniture then lives in people's homes.

The flowers and leaves to be collected for the book marker should be no bigger than 3.3cm (about an inch and a half) in diameter. Lay the flowers and leaves flat between the pages of the book. Each child will need at least five flowers and five leaves. Take the opportunity to remind the children that they should never take flowers from people's gardens or parks without permission. Bring the book back home or to school and put it on the floor with other books, or a brick, on top for weight. Write the date of collection on a piece of paper and leave it on top. In three weeks the flowers will be pressed and ready for use. You will find instructions for making the book markers on page 76.

Bits of tree bark, fir cones, very dry leaves, bits of stick, etc, can be collected to put in the Easter Garden. Moss and stones might also be found on this trip for the Easter Garden.

Point out signs of Spring to the children, new growth in plants and leaf buds on the trees. Encourage them to look under sticks and stones for worms and other such life. There is a sense of new life and hope in Springtime to match the sense of new life and hope we have because of the events of Easter.

An Easter Garden

As the crib is to Christmas, the garden is to Easter. It is an imaginative recreation in symbols of the events of Easter Week. As the children construct the garden during the weeks of lent, they will be kept in mind of the story of Jesus and of how he died for us and rose again on Easter Sunday. They will be reminded of how Jesus loves us, listens to us, helps us and is our friend; of how some people love him and others turn away from him. Because of this, we have the chance to show our love for him by helping other people.

The Easter Garden will take six weeks to build if you concentrate on a different aspect each week. The making of the papier maché tomb and the figures will take the longest time.

The foundation of the garden

> *Materials:*
> Waterproof ground cover
> Green cloth, wood chippings or moss
> Bricks or small cardboard boxes
> Large stones for rockery effect
> A piece of mirror for a lake

Find a floor space in a corner of a room, or a table, on which to construct the garden. Cover the space with a plastic or polythene sheet. This will protect against spillage when the plants are watered. Underneath the sheet, place the bricks or cardboard boxes to give an undulating effect to the terraine. Make sure to leave a flat space into which the tomb will fit. Cover the ground sheet with a green cloth, moss or wood chippings.

Foliage
Potted plants, shrubs and trees will give the garden a rich foliage effect. Place the larger plants at the back and around the sides and the smaller ones in front. Ivy is very useful for draping over things and giving the effect of age.

Ensure that you label the plants with the owner's name so that they can be returned after Easter. If you are working from a church it might be worth your while approaching the local garden centre for a loan of plants. Explain what you want them for and offer to put up a little notice near the Easter Garden giving them credit for lending the plants.

The tomb
There are several ways in which a tomb can be constructed.

(a) A papier maché tomb

> *Materials:*
> Old basin
> Newspaper scissors
> Chickenwire
> Wallpaper paste
> Wire cutters
> Stone coloured paint and brushes (optional)

Cut the chicken wire to suit the size of the garden, which can be small enough to fit on a table or large enough to fill a whole corner of a room. Bend the piece of chicken wire into a tomb shape with a space to enter. Dent the tomb here and there to give a rock effect when it is covered with papier mache.

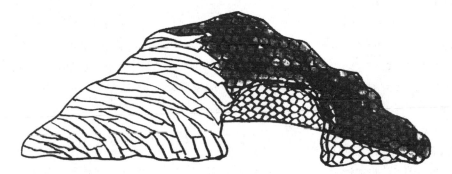

Cut the pieces of paper into strips about 5cm in width. Make up the wallpaper paste according to the instructions on the packet. Dip the paper strip by strip into the paste. Take off excess paste by running your fingers scissors-like down the strip of paper. Drape the paper strip over the chickenwire and repeat until the tomb is completely covered.

Allow to dry for a couple of days before applying the next layer. Repeat until there is a fairly thick cover on the tomb. When completely dry, the tomb can be left as it is or it could be painted in a stone colour.

(b) Cardboard Tomb

> *Materials:*
> A cardboard box
> Stiff grey paper
> Stapler or glue
> Scissors

Cut off the lose flaps around the open end of the box. Loosely scrunch up the stiff grey paper and attach it to the outside of the box with staples or glue. Bring the grey paper down over the open edges of the box to leave a half-circle opening in front of the tomb, hiding the box.

(c) A Stone Tomb

Large stones might be built up to form a cave which would serve as a tomb. The stones need to be balanced in such a way as not to cause injury to children if they collapse. Moss or ivy can be draped over the stones to give a more authentic appearance.

Backdrop (Optional)

The children might paint a hill with three crosses on top and a path coming down towards the garden. This can be used as a backdrop to the garden by pinning it to the wall behind.

Pipe Cleaner people

Materials:

Pipe cleaners	Markers
Table-tennis balls	Card from cereal packets
Wool for hair	Tin or silver foil
Glue and scissors	

Pieces of coloured tissue-paper or material

The neck and arms are made from one pipe cleaner. Bend in half, with the bent end uppermost. Twist the top half to form the neck and open out the ends for arms.

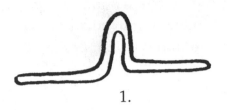

1.

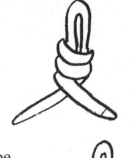

2.

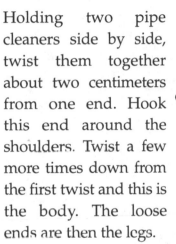

3.

Holding two pipe cleaners side by side, twist them together about two centimeters from one end. Hook this end around the shoulders. Twist a few more times down from the first twist and this is the body. The loose ends are then the legs.

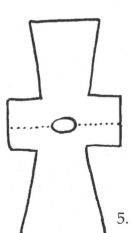

4.

Cut out a simple costume from material or coloured paper as shown in the diagram and put it on the figure before the head goes on. Using coloured tissue paper and glue to dress the pipe-cleaner people will be simpler for small children than using material.

Pierce a small hole in the table tennis ball with a sharp scissors and insert the neck of the pipe-cleaner person into it. Paint a face with the markers and glue on hair and a beard as required.

5.

The pipe-cleaner person is then fixed in a base of playdough or plasticene and you can bend them into different poses.

A long veil was the headdress for women, and either a short veil with head band or a turban was common for men. These can be held in place with straight pins or glued on.

Playdough or plasticine

Angel's Wings
Fold a card in
half and cut
out as a set

A soldier will have a cloak attached at the neck and will carry a dagger or spear and wear a helmet. Make the soldier's dress shorter and straighter and then put trimming around the waist.

The trimming

Paint the helmet and trimming grey or silver.

For the helmet, use the same kind of trimming but make it short and narrower. Double it to help it sit better and tape it underneath to hold it together before sticking it to the head.

Swords, daggers, helmets and wings can be cut out from the cereal packet card and covered in tinfoil. The wings and helmets can be glued on, while the swords and daggers will be gripped in the hand by wrapping the end of the pipe cleaner around the handle.

The Tomb Stone

This is made by cutting a circle of card to fit over the opening of the tomb. Cover the card with papier maché, or scrunched-up stiff grey paper, to make it look like a big rock.

Stone slab

This will be placed in the tomb to lay the body of Jesus on. Make it from a box, ranging in size from a matchbox upwards to suit the size of the tomb. Cover it with papier maché or paint it grey.

Other ideas

Lots of little animals and insects can be added to the garden by the children, eg. ladybirds, butterflys, birds, rabbits etc. and some could be half hidden in the foliage to make a game – 'How many butterflys can you spot?'

Taking care of the garden

All the items in the garden must be cared for regularly, as most of them will be on loan. Appoint a different child to water the plants each week.

Getting the most from the garden

Those with Easter Gardens at home, or in their local church, can celebrate the events of Easter as they happen. On Good Friday evening, the body of Jesus is place on the slab in the tomb. The body is wrapped in a white grave-cloth. The big stone is rolled across the door to prevent anyone stealing the body. There will be some soldiers, apostles and women in the garden that evening. When the children come down on Holy Saturday morning, all the people will have gone from the garden and the stone will be in place at the entrance of the tomb. The children will probably peep to see if the body of Jesus is still there.

When the children get up on Easter Sunday morning, they will find the stone rolled to one side and Jesus' body gone. The women will be in the garden with the two angels. As the day goes on, other people will come to look. There will be Mary Magdalene, Mary the mother of James and Joanna, along with soldiers and other disciples.

Themes

Jesus is our friend

Jesus made friends with all the unimportant people. Lepers were called unimportant people. Nobody wanted to be near them or to touch them. But Jesus loved the lepers very much. He went up to a leper, reached out and touched him, and wanted to be his friend.

He was friendly with some rich people too, some important people. Jesus was friendly with these people, not because of their power and wealth, but because of the love in their hearts.

A friend is someone who is interested in you for yourself. A friend is someone with whom you enjoy playing, talking or working. Jesus is our friend, because even when we forget him, or are annoyed with him, he is still our friend. He never falls out with us. He just waits for us to be friendly with him again.

Jesus is a very faithful friend.

Related resources:
Story: Friends, page 32
Prayers: page 50
Colouring picture: Jesus and the children, page 90

Jesus listens to us

I can share my most wonderful and deepest thoughts with Jesus. He listens to me all the time.

When I'm sad or angry I can always talk to Jesus, my friend.

Because he is my friend, he knows if I'm happy or sad, frightened or brave. When I'm happy I want to tell him because I know he will be happy for me too. When I'm in trouble and things are going wrong for me, I ask him to help me to be brave and to face the problem.

My Mam and my Dad listen to me, and my friends listen to me sometimes too. My special friend Jesus is always there to listen. It's great to have a friend like Jesus who never gets tired of me.

Related resources:
Story: Listening with the heart, page 36
Prayers: page 51

Jesus helps us

Jesus wants us to build a new world. We build the new world when we help each other. We build the new world when we share together and have fun together.

Our parents love us, and so they also are building the new world. Our teachers help us in the classroom and in the playground. Doctors and nurses build the new world by helping people all the time in hospitals.

Jesus loves to see people building the new world. Jesus sends the Holy Spirit to encourage us to build the new world at home and at school and wherever we are.

Related resources:
Story: Building a new world, page 38
Prayers: page 52

Jesus loves us

When I think of the people who love me, like my parents and grandparents, aunts and uncles, brothers and sisters, it makes me feel warm and safe.

Jesus tells us about God's great love for us. He tells us that God's love is very deep and strong and that makes me feel warm and safe too.

Sometimes we turn our back on God's love. We walk away from him when we are mean or selfish. But Jesus says that he is always waiting for us to come back. Jesus says that God's love for us never changes, no matter what we do.

Jesus says that God loves us even more than we could imagine.

Related resources:
Story: At Peace, page 41
Prayers: page 53

Jesus forgives us

Zacchaeus loved money more than anything else. He made people pay more than they should. He was very selfish.

Then he heard, from lots of people, what Jesus was saying about building the new world. He began to wonder. He realised that what he was doing was not building the new world.

Zacchaeus went to listen to Jesus as soon as he could. When he heard what Jesus had to say about loving and caring for each other, he decided to change his ways.

Zacchaeus invited Jesus to his house to tell him exactly how he was going to change his ways. Jesus praised him in front of all the people and gave him God's forgiveness.

When we go to Confession, we tell the priest how we are changing our ways. He gives us God's forgiveness.

Related resources:
Story: A Change of heart, page 43
Prayers: page 54

Jesus shows us the way to live

Jesus was tempted, just as we are sometimes. He heard the voice of the devil telling him to look after himself, enjoy himself, and forget about everybody else. 'Don't even give them a thought!' But Jesus was having none of it.

The devil then tempted Jesus to become a big boss, to become the most important man in the world. He could then push everybody around, without a care for anyone's feelings. But Jesus was having none of it.

Eventually the devil gave up and went away.

When we are tempted, we know that Jesus understands. He knows how hard it is for us. Jesus wants us to say in our hearts, 'I'll have none of it!'

Jesus shows us the way.

Related resources:
Story: A home for 401, page 45
Prayers: page 55

Stories

Friends

Related Theme: Jesus is our friend page 24

We lived on the island. In the summer we played in the sea and tumbled in the waves. We splashed each other in the shallow water and then it was helter skelter into the sand dunes for more fun. The shouts of children racing and playing was a kind of music that filled the air.

And in the summer it was easy to travel over to the mainland. We'd pile into a boat and we'd row over, do our shopping, have a day out and in the evening row back home again to the island. In the winter it was often cold and windy. On some winter nights a storm blew. You could hear the howl of it. The sea, too, seemed to get into a rage and hurl itself, over and over again, at the rocks that stood out on the shore. Each time the sea rushed in, there was a a sound like an explosion. The sea tried to drown the rocks in foaming water and cover them over. But each time the water had to roll back and let the rocks come to the surface again. It was a fight to the death between angry giants but neither side ever seemed to win. It was quiet for a minute until the sea gathered up its strength for the next rush against the rocks. And the rocks waited to smash the sea into a million sprays of water. I was glad to be in the house near the warm fire.

It was a wild night like that when word came to our house that Widow Mc Bride's child was very sick. My mother put on a heavy coat and a shawl and went up the road to be with her neighbour, and offer what help she could. The news wasn't good. It sounded like appendicitis. And it was said that appendicitis, without a hospital operation, could kill. My dad said it was too stormy to bring out a boat. There was nothing for it but to call out the lifeboat and get the child into hospital. The lifeboat was called out from the mainland and we all waited. The child was got ready and dressed.

We walked close together down to the pier, heads and shoulders bent into the wind and rain. Dawn was breaking when the lifeboat was spotted, bobbing up and down on the rough seas heading towards the island. The storm had, if anything, got worse. To get into our pier you had come from the open sea through a narrow straight that was bounded on both sides by rocks. In a storm you had to keep the line of your boat very true or risk being pulled against the rocks on one side or the other. A single rock would gash your boat and sink you in a second. The lifeboat slowed down outside the straight. The waves were mountainous. The lifeboat came forward very slowly into the straight but almost immediately reversed back out into the open sea. The straight was too dangerous. The lifeboat wasn't able to land. The lifeboatmen tried to manoeuvre into the straight four or five times and each time they had to back off. Finally they pulled out in the open sea, anchored and waited for the sea to get calmer.

But Widow Mc Bride's child couldn't wait. She was very ill and needed to be in hospital. She could be dead within a few hours. My mother looked at my father. We were the best boat men on the island. We won first prize at regattas in Galway and Donegal. There was nothing about boats we didn't know. 'I'll take out the small boat,' my father said, 'and bring the sick child out to the lifeboat.' 'It could be the saving of the child.' 'John will row in front,' he said. John was my brother and he was nineteen. 'And Katie will hold the child in the middle of the boat' – that was me and I was just turned sixteen – 'and I'll row from the back,' said my father, 'and guide the boat through the waves.'

The boat was brought down from where it was stored and put

into the water in a shallow sheltered spot. Many willing hands held the boat steady. My brother John got in first and settled himself into his place at the front. I sat in the middle and Widow Mc Bride gave me her child into my lap. The woman's eyes were fearful with worry. I cradled the child against the storm and the water and settled into my place. My mother was crying. Then my father sat in. John and himself began to row into the waves as if they were one person. They were completely in tune. Every stroke of the oars backwards and forwards was in perfect rhythm. We climbed each huge wave. When we sat at the top of the waves I could see the rocks on either side being lashed by the sea. I felt they were waiting to destroy us. Then down we went into the trough just like a cork and up again. The wind was howling. There was noise everywhere. And rain. It was horrible. I thought one really mountainous wave was going to topple us. We hung in the air for what seemed like forever and then we were gliding free into the next wave. It was only a hundred yards down the straight into the open sea but it was the longest hundred yards of my life.

We got to the mouth of the straight where the lifeboat was waiting. A lifeboatman was hanging out over the side wearing tackle. His plan was to lift the child to safety when we came alongside the lifeboat. My father got our boat into position and we made our run. Up we went on a wave alongside the lifeboat. The lifeboatman grabbed the child and swung her to safety. I let the child go. I didn't move a muscle because in a small boat you don't move even an inch because you could throw the boat out of balance and cause disaster. We turned round in a wide, safe circle and headed back into the straight. What we had done going out, we did coming back. Rhythm, care, and perfect seamanship.

When we got into the shallow safe water and the end of the pier there was a crowd cheering us. Even the wind didn't drown those cheers. Widow Mc Bride hugged me and wouldn't let me go. My mother was smiling. My father was saying, 'I want Katie at the next Regatta in Galway. She has the beating of any man!" We all went back to our house for bread and tea and talk. No one went home till it was morning that night.

And needless to say, the news from the hospital was good. The child was over the operation and out of danger.

Listening with the heart

Related Theme: Jesus listens to us page 25

When he was born, his mother knew there was something wrong. He lay just a little too limp in her arms. The tests in the hospital confirmed it. He had a weakness of the body muscles. This also affected his vocal chords. He would never be able to speak, and all his movements would be limp and uncontrolled.

His mother was devastated. But she quickly grew out of her disappointment. Instead she developed a fierce love for her handicapped son.

As the days and the months passed, she became convinced that her son was gifted. She believed that his talents were hidden because he had no voice to tell anyone what he wanted to say.

She read to him, stories and more stories. He seemed to drink them all in. She knew he was enjoying it all. Then it was poetry. After poetry came music. Every kind of music.

People wondered why she was doing all this. Did he need all this education to enjoy a narrow little life in a wheelchair. 'He needs it,' she said, 'because he wants it. He wants the challenge. He wants to understand everything, to know everything that can be known. I listen to him. He can't speak but I can hear him. We talk together,' she said. 'We have our own language. I can share his thoughts.' She laughed, 'Our chemistry clicks!'

But the boy could never go to school. He couldn't speak, and writing words and sentences was an impossible problem. He had no control over the muscles in his arms or fingers. Holding and guiding a pencil was beyond him. But he did have control over the muscles of his neck and head. She strapped a pencil to his head and the first lessons in writing began. It was slow work. She sensed that he loved every minute of it. She was in tune with his feelings. Someone gave him a present of a computer. The pencil on his head tapped the electronic keys and he was writing: words, sentences, paragraphs. People who know about these things said the quality of his writing was quite exceptional for his age. When he was ten, he wrote a poem that was read out in a University class. The boy was indeed gifted. His mother was right. She had heard the call of the spirit of creativity that was imprisoned in his broken body and had worked and worked to set it free. In his darkness she heard a voice asking her to open a door into a world of words and thoughts and endless dreams. And what a struggle it was to open that door. But they swung it open together.

He is a teenager now. They are both doing the Open University Course on his computer. He helps her with assignments! There are a few doors he can open for her, too.

Building a new world

Related Theme: Jesus helps us page 26

They lived near the desert. A small community. Fruit and crops were plentiful enough when the rain fell, but that wasn't very often. Water was a constant worry. They had a well but it wasn't deep enough. The well had dried up more than once in the last five years. Animals died and crops shrivelled in the fields. The people managed to survive by dragging water from another well two miles away. Next time it could be a real disaster.

A deeper well was needed. Everyone was agreed on that. A government engineer had visited their community and said a drilling rig would be sent to bore a deeper well. The community were on the list. But nothing ever happened.

After the last drought they decided to do something themselves. A delegation was elected to go to the city to plead with the Council for Development for a drilling rig. The delegation prepared for the meeting and the journey, and went off to the city. They walked up to the great city hall. After a long time they got to speak to a manager from the Council for Development. Even while they were speaking he was shaking his head. A drilling rig was not possible in the near future. Maybe later on. Too few drills, too many communities. They would have to wait. He said he would do his best, and bade them good day.

They went home and told a disappointed community the news that their pleas for a drilling rig were not successful. The community was not prepared to accept this bad news. The delegation were sent back to the city to plead again. This time they argued their case with the manager more strongly. They felt more confident. They were assured their community was on a list. Maybe next year the drill would come. It sounded like a hollow promise. It was no good.

When the community heard that their pleas had fallen on deaf ears, they decided that everyone should go and plead the case with the Council for Development. They made their way, men, women and children, to the city hall and filled it. The Manager was very taken aback. He got angry and told them all to go home. He could do nothing for them, he said. They made it clear they weren't leaving until they got a drilling rig. They would prefer to die, they said, from exhaustion in the city hall rather than die from thirst in their own fields. They stayed all night in the square outside the building. Next morning they were back in the hall again pleading their case. The Senior Manager heard the commotion. What was going on! All these country people filling the city hall! A disgrace! And the newspapers were beginning to ask questions. Photographers were arriving. The country people were already being interviewed. A story with the wrong slant could look bad for the Council for Development. The Senior Manager held a press conference at which he announced that the Council for Development were glad to be able to help the community whose people were present making their case. A drilling rig would be on its way the very next day.

After a few days a great truck arrived at the community fitted out with a drilling rig. Drilling began in earnest. The steel bit dug into the ground. Round and round it spun, twisting deeper into the soil. It bored right down into the hard stony ground all that day and the next day. Deeper and deeper. There was a buzz of excitement when the ground around the bore-hole became soggy and wet. They had finally reached the underground reservoir. But still they drilled. Another four metres. Now the water began to flow, first a trickle, then a steady little stream. At last the community had water that wouldn't go away in the first dry spell.

The men in the truck packed away their gear and headed back to the city. The whole community of men, women and children gathered round the bore hole. The sides of the new well were tiled with flat stones. A wall was built.

They made a ceremony of thanksgiving for water and for their new well.

At Peace

Related Theme: Jesus loves us page 27

Jonathan was into his twenties and he was in love. His future wife was a perfect partner for him. They got on really well together and enjoyed each other's company and each other's talk. The day for the wedding was settled. They were going to live in a new home and raise a family. They didn't have much money but they had a precious diamond ring which would pay for a house and give them a start with their new business.

Jonathan's younger brother would stay on in the family house. The two brothers had lived together since their parents died in the Great Plague. The brothers were very close but they had both grown up and it was time for separation. Each one would go their own way.

The Church was booked for Jonathan's wedding and the marriage feast was planned down to the last detail. But the plans were shattered when Jonathan's younger brother ran off with the diamond ring. Why did he do it? What got into him? Why did he spoil his older brother's future plans? There were no answers. Someone said that his younger brother was deeply unhappy, that he felt a failure in life and was envious of the love and good fortune his older brother seemed to enjoy. Perhaps he had to get away from it all.

Jonathan was angry at first but, as the days passed, he became concerned about his brother. His future wife assured him that the ring wasn't everything. 'It would have made things easier for us,' she said, 'but you and I have a closeness that's more important than money.' They postponed the wedding date. She encouraged Jonathan to think about going and looking for his brother. 'He needs your love,' she said. 'You were always very close. Maybe he saw our marriage as a great loss for him, a separation from you that he couldn't face. You were such good friends. He couldn't face the break up of his friendship with you.'

Jonathan took her advice and went off to the city in search of his younger brother. He visited pubs and ale-houses, building sites and boarding houses, always asking for news of his brother. One day he found him. He met him by pure chance in the street. At first the younger brother was very embarrassed but Jonathan made it clear that he wasn't coming for the ring. He cared about his brother. They went together to a coffee house and talked all that evening. The ring was indeed gone. Sold for half its value and the money squandered. But the younger brother was settled into a job and there was a girl at work who smiled at him. Maybe he would ask her out.

Jonathan went home to his future wife and told her what had happened. 'I'm coming up with you next week,' she said, 'to meet your brother. I want to assure him that I care about him too.' The three of them met the next week. She invited him home for the wedding. 'I want you to be our best man,' she said. 'I won't come between you and your brother. You need each other still. You can be the most wonderful of friends.'

The younger brother did come home for the wedding. It was a smaller wedding than was planned. Jonathan and his wife didn't buy a house. They rented one. He didn't start the new business that year. His younger brother and himself decided they would wait for a year, save money and go into it together.

Jonathan's wife was delighted the two brothers were at peace again.

A Change of Heart

Related Theme: Jesus forgives us page 28

He was a scoundrel. He loved to lend money, and get it all back with big interest. Most of the people that he lent money to were poor and needy. He had them by the throat. They had to borrow to live.

He loved buying things from alcoholics or drug addicts. They wanted money so badly to feed their habits that they offered quite valuable items at less than half-price. And if a widow was left running a farm after her husband's death, he would offer her a tidy sum for farm and stock to save her all the trouble, or so he said. It was sometimes hard to resist the offer of money. And it was always a deal that favoured him out and out. A bargain for him. A loss for everyone else.

When there was famine in the land he sold food at blackmarket prices. When there was drought he had water for sale. He was called a rat, a thief, a conniving devil, a grave robber. He didn't seem to mind. He continued to build up his fortune.

He visited a cabin one day after a death to see if there was a bargain going. During the visit he felt unwell and got weak. He fell ill with the very disease that had swept away the much-loved man of the place. The mother and two children knew the sort of their visitor, knew he was despised, knew he was low and mean. They knew he came to their house to offer them what he called 'a bargain' in their distress, but no matter. They tended to him in his sickness. They wiped the perspiration from his brow and tried to cool the fever that was killing him. When they thought he was able to take it, they gave him a few spoons of water on his lips and then a little soup on his tongue. Every day for a week they nursed him. The fever passed. He survived and was ready to go home. And when he was leaving they gave him flowers.

What happened in the little house, where his life was saved by three brave women, changed him completely. He had experienced a special kind of love and tenderness. It melted his hard heart. It touched him and changed him. He changed his ways. People thought he was up to new tricks. It took time for people to be convinced that he really had changed. But changed he had. He became a community person. He showed signs of caring. He took an interest in people.

He really did change his ways. And, for what it was worth, he did try to make amends.

A home for 401

Related Theme: Jesus shows us the way to live page 29

His name was 401. A stray dog. There was no name on his collar. Or if there was, it had been torn off. Just the numbers 401 scrawled in pencil.

He came to them at night. It was a very wet night. Their father heard the whining in the garden shed, shone the torch and there he was: wet, cold, shivering, and undernourished. He was brought into the house, warmed up, washed, fed and made comfortable. He enjoyed the attention. An English Cocker Spaniel with brown and white colouring. It was fun having a visitor. The next day they went to the police station to tell their story. There were no reports of a missing Cocker Spaniel. They went to their local vet to tell him but again he had no news about a missing dog of that breed.

401 came to stay with the family and became a favourite pet. Mary was the one who took to him, brought him for walks in the park, fed him and played with him. 401 chased after balls, retrieved sticks from ponds and was a 'natural' in the sea. At first, Mary imagined that they would find his owner but, as the months passed, he just became part of the family. Mary became very attached to him. Her other dog had been killed in a traffic accident and 401's arrival was a kind of miracle. It filled a gap in her life.

It was a terrible shock when Mary happened to see a notice in the corner of their newspaper which read:

'His name is 401. English Cocker Spaniel. Missing in

Ireland for a year now. His birthday is today. Much missed by Gladys. Information to this telephone number in Wales.'

What was Mary to do? Tell her parents? Ring Gladys in Wales? She was going to lose 401. That was for sure. And she couldn't let that happen. 401 was in a good home. He was settled in. Mary felt like a parent who has to give back an adopted child. She said nothing. Didn't mention a word of the newspaper item to anyone at home, even to her best friend at school.

Maybe they could all forget about it. 401 was happy and that was all that mattered. Returning 401 now would upset him. It wouldn't be right. He would be torn between two masters. At this stage he would surely have forgotten Gladys. All the thoughts for and against sending 401 back to Wales twisted around in her mind. She did nothing about it. 401 was staying! Mary was keeping him. The thought of the newspaper item would have to be forgotten and lost in her mind. 401 was hers now and she would protect him.

When she was in the park one day, 401 was being particularly playful. Mary thought of Gladys in Wales. She hoped Gladys loved 401. The girl in Wales must really be fond of 401 if she was still looking for him a year after he went missing. She decided to get in touch. It wasn't easy. Mary's dad did the phoning. It turned out that Gladys's family had been on holiday in Ireland and their much loved 401 had been stolen. That was how he came to Mary's family. He must have escaped from his captors. The memories of the night they found him hiding in the garden shed came back. He might have run miles and miles in those days when he escaped.

It was interesting that Mary and Gladys were the same age. 401 had found a new master that was the image of Gladys.

Gladys's family arrived from Wales. Jones was their family

name. They were made very welcome. Gladys and Mary took 401 out to the park. He took to Gladys straight away but always ran back to Mary. Both girls cried a little. It was a joyful time for Gladys and heartbreak time for Mary. It was nice the Joneses were able to stay for the weekend. They were a lovely family. It gave Mary a chance to be reassured that 401 would be alright back in his first home in Wales. But it was a separation that made her feel lonely and empty. It wasn't easy. There was a gap in her life when 401 went away.

It was only after a few weeks passed that she was glad she followed up on the newspaper ad. It wouldn't have been right to ignore it. It wouldn't have been right to keep 401 from Gladys. And she had 401's company for a whole year. That was something to be thankful for.

Mary and Gladys are pen pals. The latest news from Wales is that Gladys has promised Mary a pup, a daughter to 401. Mary is very excited at the thought.

Prayers

Prayers: Friends

Dear God,
Thank you for my friends,
especially for my best friend.
Help me to be friends
with the children in my class who get left out. Amen

Mums and Dads are special friends,
brothers and sisters too.
Help us to be friends to them
In everything we do. Amen. *Amy R. 3 yrs.*

I like to think of Jesus as a happy friend,
I like to think of Jesus every now and then.
I like to show him lots of love
by being a good friend too. Amen. *Kiara 9 yrs.*

Prayers: Listening

Dear God,
Help me to listen at Mass.
Help me to listen to the priest.
Help me to listen to your word,
because I know
that you speak with love. Amen. *James 9 yrs.*

Dear God,
Help me to listen to all the beautiful sounds
in your world,
the sounds of the city,
the sounds of the countryside,
the sounds of the sea.
Thank you, God our Father,
for all the beautiful sounds
in your world. Amen

Dear God,
Jesus wants us to listen to our friends.
He also wants us to listen to people
who are not our friends.
This is sometimes not easy.
Help us, God our Father. Amen

Prayers: Helping

Dear God,
Help me to build a new world of love. Amen

Dear God,
Many people are helping to build a new world,
my parents, teachers, lollipop lady, shopkeepers,
postmen, priests, nurses, policemen and my friends.
Bless them all and keep them safely in your care. Amen.

God our Father,
I thank you for my life,
for books and toys and friends.
If I could not play games
with my friends I would feel sad.
Thank you, God our Father. Amen. *John 9 yrs.*

Dear God,
I would like to do something helpful everyday.
Please help me to look out for someone who needs my help.
Amen.

Prayers: Loving

Thank you, God, for being kind and caring.
Thank you for Jesus, our friend.
Thank you, God, for loving me and my family.
I love you too. Amen. *Kim 9 yrs.*

Thank you, God, for the earth,
the birds, the trees and all the bees,
But most of all for me. Amen. *Tony 9 yrs.*

Dear God,
Jesus asks us to show love.
Help us to show love by making people happy,
by inviting people to join in our games.
by doing chores without being asked,
by being friendly and kind and helpful. Amen.

Prayers: Forgiving

God our Father,
You gave us kindness and a heart full of love.
You give us the gift of forgiving.
Help us to forgive people who get on our nerves
just as you forgive us. Amen. *Amy F. 9 yrs.*

Dear God,
Jesus asks us to forgive.
He says this is the way to build a new world.
Help us to have a spirit of forgiveness. Amen.

Dear God,
Forgiveness is needed at home and at school
and in the playground.
May the gift of forgiveness
always find a place in our hearts. Amen.

Prayers: The New Way

The new way
is the way of love and kindness
and consideration for our family and our friends.
Dear God our Father,
help us to live in the new way. Amen.

Dear God our Father,
I helped my Mammy when she was sick.
I got messages for my Daddy.
I comforted my dog when she was going to die.
Thank you, God, for helping me
to live in the new way. Amen. *Vallen 10 yrs.*

Dear God,
Jesus lived in the new way.
He showed kindness to the outsiders,
to those who were lonely or despised.
He forgave his enemies.
Help me to follow Jesus
and live in the new way. Amen.

Games

The backwards obstacle race

The children divide up into pairs for this game. If there are a lot of children, the pairs can be divided up into six or eight teams. There must be a volunteer to lay out the obstacles for each team.

In each pair, one child acts as guide while the other child walks backwards avoiding a series of obstacles.

The walking child stands facing the guide at one end of the room while a third child lays out the obstacles behind him or her, e.g. a cushion, a magazine, a chair, some skittles, bean bags, hoops etc.

The guide then talks the walking child through the obstacle path to the other end of the room. The walking child runs back up the room, swops places with the guide, and the obstacles are changed again.

If the walking child looks back while on the obstacle path, s/he is out and must start again. If s/he bumps into an item s/he loses a point.

The game can be played in a non-competitive fashion, simply as an exercise in trusting.

Whichever way it is played, the children will enjoy it and there is a lesson to be learned.

Chinese Whispers

Write a short message on a piece of paper. For example:
> Mary's granny baked a cake for Mary's birthday. The baby climbed up on the table and stuck his finger in the icing.

or
> The little boy got sick at night and his mammy took him to the hospital. The car broke down on the way.

Sit the children in a circle. Pick one child in the circle and give the message to him/her in a whisper. That child whispers the message to the child on the left, who whispers it to the next child, and so on to the end of the circle. When the last child recieves the message ask him/her to call it out. Compare this message with the first child's message and with what is written down. Note the way the message was distorted in the telling.

Discussion:
How did the message get changed?
What is a rumour?
Have you ever heard a rumour?
If you heard a rumour would you believe it?

Co-operation game

Using fairly strong card, cut out six rectangles all the same size. It will be slightly easier for the children to play the game if the back of the card is a different colour from the front. On the front of the cards, draw outlines for cutting the cards into different shapes (see the diagram for examples). In the set of six there must not be two shapes exactly the same. Cut the cards into shapes and, before they get mixed up, lightly mark each piece with a number, letter or symbol on the back which will allow you to piece them together quickly. It is not intended that the children should see these marks.

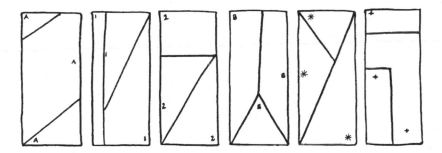

Take six large envelopes and place three shapes in each, making sure that there are no matching marks in any one envelope. Divide the children into groups of three or four. Before you mix up the pieces, you will need to know how many groups of children you have as you need one complete rectangle per group.

Each group is given an envelope of mixed pieces and the game begins. To make a complete rectangle they have to interact with the other groups. They cannot ask for a piece from another group. They cannot steal a piece. They cannot indicate in any way that they need a piece. They must wait for another group to offer them a piece which they can accept or refuse. The idea is that they will notice what the other groups need, and offer it to them.

Discussion:

How did you feel when you saw another group with your piece and you couldn't ask for it?

Were you worried that you wouldn't get your rectangle completed?

Were you tempted to keep all your pieces in case you needed them?

Were you tempted to keep all your pieces to prevent someone else finishing before you?

Did it feel good when others were generous to you?

Mime it

The children are divided up into teams of four or six. A leader is picked by each team. The leaders are given a message written on a piece of paper, or they are taken outside the door and the message is given verbally, a different message for each team. The leader then mimes the message to his or her own team. No words are allowed.

The first team to get the message is the winner, but let the game continue until all the teams have got it.

Suggestions for messages:
> Make a cup of tea.
> Do your home-work.
> Make your bed.
> Turn off the television.
> Cut the grass.
> It's time to go to bed.

The game can be played several times so that each child in the team gets a chance to be the leader and do the mime.

Teasing tangle

For this game you need children with patience and the ability to take instruction. An even number of children, preferably more than four, form a circle shoulder to shoulder. One child is picked as a leader. The children close their eyes, put their right hand into the circle and catch another hand. Now, put the left hand into the circle and catch another hand. Now they can open their eyes and without letting go of hands they must get themselves out of the tangle. The leader's job is to talk them out of the mess, otherwise there will be chaos. The children will have great fun scrambling over arms and legs until the circle is formed again.

Discussion:
What did it feel like to follow the instructions of your leader?
Did you think you'd never get out of the tangle?
Were you tempted to cheat and let go of hands?
At what other time would you have to follow instructions carefully?

Wink murder

This game needs ten or more players. The children sit in a circle. Take one child outside the door. While he/she is outside, pick one child in the circle to be the murderer.

The first child is brought in and sits in the centre of the circle. His/her job is to be detective and to catch the murderer before too many children are killed. When the murderer winks at a child, the child drops down dead and stays dead until the end of the game.

Only the murderer is allowed to wink and it is by catching someone winking that the detective will know he/she has caught the murderer. If the murderer manages to kill everyone in the circle, he/she gets to be detective for the next round. Otherwise two new people are picked.

This game needs no words and it can be quite difficult for some children to admit they have been winked at and they may refuse to die.

Crafts

Stainglass picture

Materials:
White paper
Pencils
Rubber
Paints and markers
Dinner plates or compas
Brushes
Cooking oil
Newspaper
Cellotape and scissors.

Take a sheet of white paper, place a dinner plate upside down on the paper and pencil a circle around the plate. Remove the plate. With a compas or smaller dinner plate, pencil an inner circle about half a centimeter in from the first circle. In the centre of the inner circle, draw a large cross and in the centre of the cross draw a dove.

Fill the space between the cross and the inner circle with odd shapes to resemble the pieces of stainglass. Colour these shapes in vibrant colours with either markers or paints. It will take a few days to complete the task as each colour must dry before applying another colour next to it. When the painting is complete, outline the colours in black.

Outline the cross and the dove in black and paint the space between the outer and inner circles in black. Allow to dry.

Now, turn the picture over and, with a clean brush and a little cooking oil, paint the whole picture on the wrong side. Place the picture between sheets of newspaper to soak up the excess oil and leave overnight.

When dry, cut around the outer circle and tape the picture to a window-pane. Once you have the idea, you can use all sorts of shapes and designs for your own stainglass windows.

Easter candles

Materials:
Old candle ends or packets of candle wax
Candle wick or thin cotton shoe laces
Small glass jars with wide necks
An old saucepan
Newspaper to protect against spillage
A fork
Cellotape and scissors
Pencils
Scented oil (Optional)
Glass Paint (optional)

Wash and dry the jars thoroughly. Tie one end of a piece of wick around the centre of a pencil. Place the pencil over the top of the

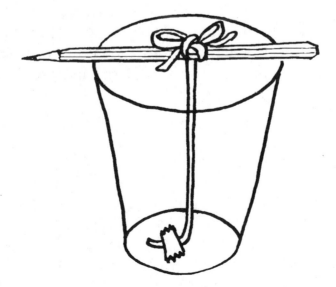

jar with the wick dropping down the centre. Cut the wick so that the end of it can be stuck to the bottom of the jar with a piece of cellotape.

Melt the old candle ends over a low heat in the saucepan. Keep the same colours together as mixed colours will come out a murkey grey or blue depending on the dominant colour. When the wax is melted, pick out the old wicks. Allow the wax to cool a little. Add a few drops of scented oil to the melted wax and stir.

With a steady hand pour the melted wax into the jar, filling it as high as you wish. Make sure the wick is coming straight up from the bottom of the jar. Leave to cool and set. As the wax sets it will shrink and a well will form in the centre of the candle. Heat a little more wax in the saucepan and pour it into the well until the top of the candle is level. Allow to set.

Take off the pencil and trim the wick. The outside of the glass can now be painted if you wish.

Because of the hot wax, this activity must be closely supervised and is better done in groups of four or six.

A Grace box

This is an idea which will encourage us to pray before meals. To say a prayer when we sit down to eat makes the occasion very special. We remember the many meals Jesus had with the people he visited. We remember God's goodness to us and the generosity of nature. When we think about the food we eat, we realise that it comes from the fields, the orchards and the animals. We think of all the people who have no food and know that, if we lived as God has planned, there would be no hungry people. We would all share what we had because God provided enough for everyone. So, even if your family doesn't usually say grace, I'm sure now is a good time to start.

First make your grace box.

> *Materials:*
> Large cereal packet or piece of stiff card.
> Scissors
> Ruler
> Glue
> Pen
> White/coloured typing paper
> Clear contact
> Paper clips

Cut the cereal packet down one side and flatten it out. Mark out a T form as in the diagram. Ensure that the measurements are correct to give you an 8cm square box with 1cm flaps. You can adjust the measurements all round to give you a larger or smaller box.

Mark in the cutting lines and folding lines on the T. Cut out the T form and cut out to release the flaps. Bend at all folding lines so that the white side of your card forms the outside of your grace box.

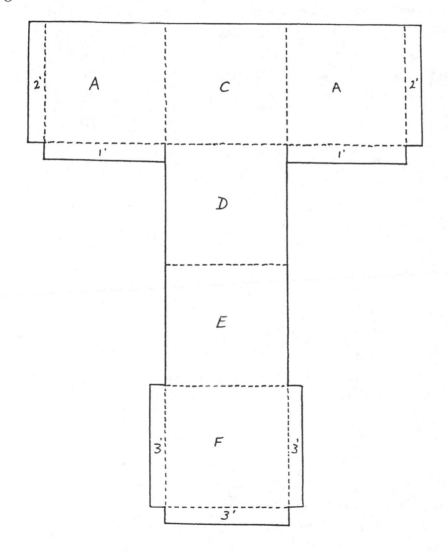

Without removing the backing from the clear contact, mark it out in a T form the same as for the card, cut out and release flaps.

With the right side of the T form card down, bend up the flaps at 1, bend in the squares at A and bend back the top square at C. Apply glue to the right sides of the flaps at 1 and stick to square D, keeping the flaps inside the box. Hold in position with paper clips until dry. Turn in the flaps at 2, apply glue, turn up the square at E and stick. Allow to dry. Glue the right side of the three flaps at 3, bend the square at F over the top of the box to form the final side. Tuck the flaps inside the box and stick. Allow to dry.

By allowing the glue to dry at each stage, it makes the box easier to handle while making it. Now cut out six circles of white or coloured paper, 7cm in diameter. Write a short grace or blessing on each. Make them up yourself, or see the sample prayers if you can't think of six. Stick a circle to each side of the box.

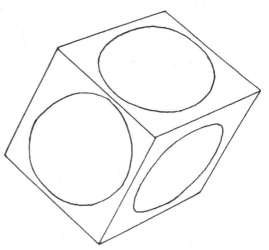

Cover the whole box with contact, removing the backing as you go along. Start by placing the box on square C, press up the sides at A, D, and E. Press flaps at 1 and 2 into position on the outside this time. Press the square at F and the flaps at 3 into position, and there you have your grace box. A lovely present to give to a family for Easter!

How to use:

Throw the box in the air and catch with both hands. The prayer nearest your right thumb is the one to read at this meal. Let a different member of the family have a turn at each meal.

Sample Prayers:

1. For food to eat
   and hands that prepare it,
   for appetites whet
   and for people to share it.
   We thank you Lord.

2. Thank you Father for this food,
   which you gave to do us good.
   Help us to remember you,
   all day long, in all we do. Amen.

3. We thank you Lord for what we've got,
   now grant us our desire.
   Remove from us the table,
   and seat us at the fire. Amen

4. Bless us O Lord and these thy gifts,
   Which of thy bounty we're about to receive,
   through Christ our Lord. Amen.

5. For food and drink and daily bread,
   we praise your name O Lord. Amen.

6. We thank you Lord for what we've got.
   Bless those who haven't any.
   We are so few, with such a lot.
   The poor, there are so many. Amen.

You will find more samples in the school religion books.

Pressed flower bookmarks

Materials:
An old telephone directory, for drying the flowers
flowers and leaves
Copydex or other quick-drying glue.
White or coloured A4 sheets of card.
Clear contact
Scissors, ruler, ribbon and hole puncher.

Cut card to the required size (I suggest 24cm x
4cm). Arrange the leaves and flowers on the
marker until you are satisfied with the
arrangement. Pick up each flower and leaf
separately and apply a small amount of copydex to the back of it and replace it. Place a
clean sheet of paper over the arrangement and
press with your hand. Remove the paper
immediately. A short message might be written beneath the flowers, especially if the
marker is to be given as a gift.

Cut a piece of clear contact 26cm x 9cm. With the sticky side facing up, peel the backing off and place the marker right side down on the contact. Press into place with your hands, making sure that the marker is in the centre of the piece of contact. Cut away the contact at the four corners as shown in diagram. Turn back the ends of the contact and press down on the back of the marker. Turn the sides of the contact onto the back of the marker and press down. The side pieces of contact will overlap.

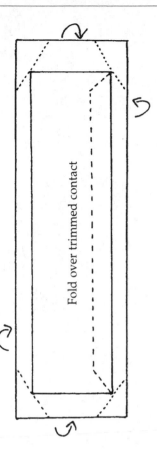

Turn the marker over and punch a hole in the centre of the bottom end and thread a piece of thin ribbon or coloured cord through and knot.

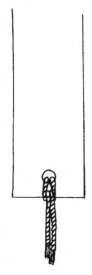

Stainglass lamps

Materials:
A strong four-fluid-ounce drinking glass
or a pretty jar with a wide neck
Glass paint in red, blue, green and yellow at least
A tube of imitation lead
Solvent (amonia or spirit depending on the paint base)
Paint brushes
Nightlights
Newspaper

A good arts and crafts shop will help you when choosing your materials, and give you advice on solvents to clean your brushes. One set of paints per class of thirty or more children will be quite sufficient when used sparingly. I have worked successfully with groups of ten children of eight years and upwards. Smaller groups are better for younger children. as they will need more individual attention.

Protect your table with news-paper. Holding the glass upside down over one hand, make patterns on the glass using the tube of lead. It takes a little practice to control the flow of lead. Fine lines of lead are as effective as thick lines and the lead lasts longer.

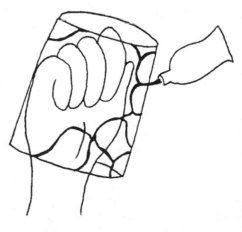

Stand the glass on newspaper for the lead to dry overnight. When painting, if you are working with several children and they have a brush each, place a pot of blue paint in front of a group of three or four, and a pot of yellow paint in front of another three or four and so on, and let them colour in all the blue patterns first etc. When they finish with one colour, they leave down their brushes and move to the next colour as a group until all the patterns have been coloured in. Individual children can move around at the end to colour in odd patterns. Paint should be used sparingly so that it doesn't run. Clean the brushes in the solvent after use.

Stand the painted glasses on newspaper overnight to dry. It is a good idea for each child to write their name on a piece of paper and drop it into the glass to avoid confusion the next day. Place a nightlight in each lamp and, taking the necessary precautions, light some of the lamps at each prayer-time.

Easter Hanging Basket

This is a delicate, decorative basket for holding sugar-coated eggs and yellow chicks or rabbits. These are a sign of hope, of new life and growth in the springtime of the year.

Materials:
A ball of knitting cotton or wool.
A balloon, scissors, glue – copydex
A length of ribbon – narrow
A length of pre-gathered lace
Two small bunches of flowers or fruit as used in hat or cake decoration
A handful of straw packing, shredded paper or cotton wool
Small yellow chickens and sugar-coated eggs or rabbits
A packet of water starch
A wooden spoon and baking bowl
Boiling and cold water

Note:
Because of the need for boiling water, this project needs close adult supervision. I suggest that the adult makes the basket with some help from small children. Older children can make it themselves in small groups with an adult.

Blow up the balloon and tie. Wet the balloon (this helps to prevent the cotton slipping). Wind the cotton or wool around the balloon to form a filigree pattern.

Following the instructions on the starch packet, make up the strongest solution described. When cool enough, dip the balloon in the solution, turning constantly to ensure the cotton/wool is thoroughly soaked. Hang out to dry, if possible, but make sure it doesn't get wet. If drying indoors, hang from the balloon tie and place a basin underneath to catch the drips. When thoroughly dry it will be stiff.

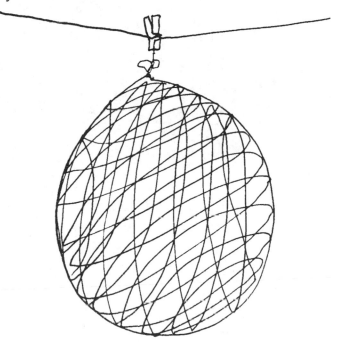

With a pin or a sharp-pointed object, puncture the balloon which will either pop and shrivel up or it will release the air and remain stuck to the sides of the basket. In either case, with your scissors, carefully cut, in the side of the basket, an oval shaped hole if you have a pear-shaped basket, or a round hole if you have a round basket. Insert your hand and gently peel the balloon from the inside (See overleaf).

Brush some glue around the edge of the hole and apply the lace all around the edge. Allow to dry.

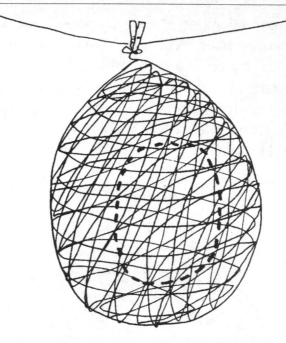

Attach bunches of flowers or fruit near the opening. Hold the decorations in place by entwining the stems through the mesh of the basket, or glue them on if they have no stems. Loop a piece of ribbon through the mesh at the top of the basket for hanging, and attach a bow here if you like.

Fill the base of the basket with a little padding and place five or six eggs in the centre with some chicks around them, or put some rabbits in. The basket can also be used to present a chocolate Easter egg in.

Warning:
If the basket gets wet or damp it will become soft and collapse. A solution of boiled sugar and water can be used to stiffen the basket if starch is not available.

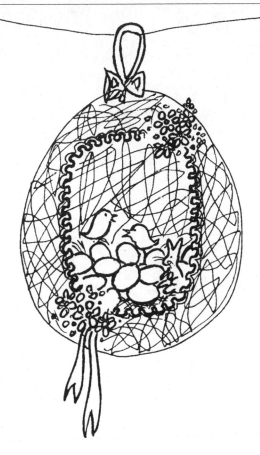

Pictures to Colour

You may like to read to the children the stories behind these pictures before they paint them. You will find them under the following references in any Bible, or it may be better to read them from your favourite children's Bible.

Daniels and Friends: Dan 2:3-25

David in Saul's armour to fight Goliath: 1 Sam 17:4-11, 34-51

Jacob tricks Isaac: Gen 27:1-37

Jesus and the elders: Lk 2:41-52

Jesus and the children: Mk 10:13-16

Jesus brings the little girl back to life: Mk 5:21-24, 35-43

You are licensed to photocopy these pictures for the children.

Daniel and friends

David in Saul's armour to fight Goliath

Jacob tricks Isaac

Jesus and the elders

Jesus and the children

Jesus brings the little girl back to life

In the same series

Step by Step through Advent
A RESOURCE BOOK FOR HOME, SCHOOL AND PARISH

Mary Fitzgerald

This is a bumper book of things to do, stories to tell, carols to sing, all designed to bring Advent to life for younger children. For each day of the four weeks of Advent, Mary Fitzgerald starts with a story (in some cases, the story goes on from one day to another) and then a verse of a carol – a new carol for each week, adding a new verse each day. After that there is a range of activities to do with the children, from making an Advent Wreath, to an Advent Calendar, to a Jesse tree, to a Christmas crib; making candles, Christmas cards and wrapping paper, and presents for Mum and Dad. There are also recipes, puppets and puzzles as well as interesting information on Christmas as it is celebrated around the world. More than enough to keep children busy and interested while learning about the meaning of Advent, either at home or in school. The book is illustrated throughout by the author.

ISBN 1 85607 111 1   112pages   £5.99
the columba press

In the same series

Colourful Children's Liturgies

Anne Marie Lee & Elaine Wisdom RCE

This is a book of simple instructions, with patterns and illustrations, on preparing a whole range of colourful visual materials for use at children's liturgies. It also contains some very useful advice on how to handle such things as story telling, mime and drama, and how to deal with the abstract themes which come up now and again in the liturgy and which have to be handled carefully if they are to be made meaningful to children.

Here you will find simple illustrated instructions for making costumes of all kinds, props for use in drama and mime, making and using various kinds of puppets, how to make and organise tableaux. There are detailed instructions on collage and making banners either on paper or with material.

ISBN 1 85607 110 3 96 pages £5.99

the columba press